IN GOD'S
PROVIDENCE:

IN GOD'S PROVIDENCE:

the birth of a Catholic Charismatic Parish

by REVEREND JOHN RANDALL

LOGOS INTERNATIONAL

Plainfield, New Jersey

LIVING FLAME PRESS

All quotations of scripture are from the *Jerusalem Bible* copyright © 1966 by Darton, Longman and Todd, Ltd., and Doubleday & Company, Inc., and are used by permission of the publisher.

Published by:

Living Flame Press/Box 74/Locust Valley, N. Y. 11560

Logos International/Plainfield, N. J. 07060
Printed in the United States of America

ISBN 0-914544-01-2

TABLE OF CONTENTS

PSALM 127

"If Yahweh does not build the house,
    in vain the masons toil;
If Yahweh does not guard the city,
    in vain the sentries watch.

In vain you get up early,
    and put off going to bed,
Sweating to make a living,
    since he provides for his beloved as they
        sleep."

IN GOD'S
PROVIDENCE:

INTRODUCTION

This book is not an overview or history of the Charismatic Renewal in the Catholic Church today. It is the tale of a specific community, a family, if you will—the Body of Christ in St. Patrick's Parish in Providence, R. I.

It is important to note that this is the story of the *birth* of a Catholic Charismatic Parish. We are discussing an infant that has not yet made a great mark on local history, an infant that has much growing to do. But nevertheless a birth has occurred and the infant is alive and healthy. Time and nurture are needed for its growth.

Throughout the last five years we have received many invitations to go to other parts of the Diocese and even across the country to share with other Charismatic groups. Unfortunately it has been necessary to decline most of them in order to stay at home and "tend the baby." But now, we want to share the life of our community with others. It is our hope that they will find the message of this book a vision of what God can do to renew a typical parish, and give hope for such renewal elsewhere.

Not all aspects of the life of our community have been covered in this book. We have hardly touched the development and interaction of the pastoral team, the Word of God Singers, the God Squad, the Healing Ministry, and the beauty the Music Ministry brings to our Liturgies and prayer meetings.

Each day's living develops the story further. The adults here are involved and we have no lack of volunteers. At one point last winter more than 500 adults were taking courses at St. Patrick's, and not one of us priests was doing the teaching. Within the individual households unique experiences are unfolding, as the Lord reveals his plans to the members. Teaching teams have gone out around New England, and farther, to bring seminars to those who could not come to us. And many have come! Some have gone home to seed groups around New England, the Eastern Seaboard, as well as in Ireland, France, Rome and Jerusalem. On one evening, a new member of the community was stunned to hear messages from a Sister from Ireland, a Bishop from Pakistan, and the Episcopal Bishop of Rhode Island at the same prayer meeting.

We have many visitors. All are welcome,

but presently we are not always able to extend the hospitality we would like. This is an area we hope to improve, using the plans we have made to accommodate the New England Regional Leaders Conference for which we were hosts in November 1973.

There are the beautiful ecumenical hopes of people of all Christian backgrounds feeling so much at home at St. Patrick's. There has been the rich contribution of the Episcopal Church of the Redeemer in Houston, Texas, a grace brought us in the visits of Rev. Graham Pulkingham, Jerry and Esther Barker, and the Fishermen. The fellowship and services we share with the Baptist and Presbyterian churches in Smith Hill have been a blessing on us all. The Capitol Hill Improvement Corporation (CHIC) is actively sponsored by all the churches. The Crafts Fair and Yard Sale, the Thanksgiving and Christmas Food Distributions, and many other joint efforts have helped build the kingdom here on Smith Hill. In addition we will be working closely with June and Ladd Fields who recently have joined Jerry and Esther Barker in establishing an East Coast Fishermen Outreach, located in Narragansett in Rev. Keith Scott's Episcopal Parish, St. Peter's By the Sea.

We hope in the near future to extend our ministry to the Chad Brown Housing Project on the edge of the parish, to complete our initial home visitations, to become as well known in our own locale as we are in many cities half a continent away, to increase our sensitivities to the wishes of those who are repelled by seemingly over-exuberant action, whether it be the kiss of peace or the singing of a hymn. We ask the Lord to increase our compassion for those who simply wish for the "good old days." But the point needs to be made that there is life; the life of Christ is among us, and it is healthy. It is a sign of hope in a dark time. This book is offered as a witness of God's presence among us and His goodness to us. Praise God.

Finally, thanks are due to so many people. To the late Bishop McVinney for the confidence he showed in launching the vision. To Bishop Gelineau who in his person has been to date more of a charismatic figure than the whole charismatic renewal in Rhode Island, for his support and reaffirmation. To Father Ray Kelly, the pastor, a faithful shepherd who is anointed to use both new ways and old in guiding the flock. To the National Catholic Renewal Services for the invaluable help it

4

offers groups throughout the country. Further thanks are due to what we consider our mother community, the Word of God in Ann Arbor, with whom we have been in constant communication since our inception. Also, particular thanks to the Church of the Redeemer. God has blessed us in our friends. To Betty Melucci and Sister Rose Alice whose self-giving and untiring hospitality has brought real harmony and order to our very busy rectory, I am grateful.

This book began as a talk I gave in November, 1972. It has subsequently been brought up to date. Thanks are due to Helen Hawkinson and Gina Boisclair without whose vision, editing and hard work this book would not have been finished.

May the Spirit of the Living God fall afresh on these pages to help fan the flames of real renewal!

Providence,
Rhode Island

Chapter I
"IN THE BEGINNING
WAS THE WORD"
THE MESSAGE: "Come and see for yourself."
John 1:39

The story of the Word of God Community in Providence, Rhode Island, really begins on a cold March day in 1967 — St. Patrick's Day to be precise. At the time, the Dioceses of Providence and Worcester were co-sponsoring a Cursillo Leaders' Workshop in Shrewsbury, Massachusetts. In the course of the workshop, Ralph Martin and Steve Clark, young national leaders in the movement, asked another priest and me if they might consult with us about a recent experience they had had at Duquesne University.

Travelling on Cursillo National Secretariat affairs, they had stopped at the Duquesne University, just a few weeks after the famous weekend that is looked upon as the birth of the Catholic Charismatic Renewal. Kevin and Dorothy Ranaghan in *Catholic Pentecostals*, and Fr. Edward O'Connor in *The Pentecostal Movement in the Catholic Church* have since described that startling and powerful time in detail, but a few words should be written now. A group of students and instructors had begun meeting to pray, study scripture, and share with each other with the object of deepening their individual prayer lives. After they gathered for a weekend "retreat" in February, 1967, one by one began to experience what is known as the Baptism in the Spirit. Ralph and Steve received the outpouring of the Holy Spirit on their visit to Pittsburgh.

They wished to talk with us because we were experienced spiritual directors. We listened to them until late into the night and were, to put it mildly, horrified. They told us of the marvelous outpouring of the charismatic gifts and we quoted St. John of the Cross who warned against spiritual excesses. We begged them, too, not to bring what they had experienced into the Cursillo Movement which was prospering, but had enough difficulties of its own. All I could think of were "Holy Rollers" and all the other perjorative terms that are associated with over-emotional religious practices. I was disillusioned and confused because prior to that, Ralph and Steve had given me such hope.

And so, to my shame and later regret, I turned off this initial opportunity to become acquainted with what was then being called the Pentecostal Movement, and for some time, totally rejected it. I've always been thankful that Ralph and Steve sought and received better advice from spiritual directors elsewhere. They remained and grew within the Charismatic movement, and serve today as national leaders of the Catholic Charismatic Renewal.

But, the sharing that March night did pique my curiosity, and from that time on, I read everything I could find about this new movement which was spreading from Duquesne to Notre Dame, to the University of Michigan, and elsewhere. Articles were beginning to appear in the *National Catholic Reporter*, *Ave Maria* and other periodicals. I was interested but I remained distant. I didn't believe that this movement could help the Cursillo or the renewal of the church in any way. I could foresee only problems we didn't need. I ignored it and went on with my regular work as spiritual director of the seminary, and continued also working with the Cursillo, with the Search Movement on the high school and college levels, and with the direction of inner city volunteer training programs.

The summer of 1967 found me plunged as deeply as ever into inner city and Cursillo work. Then one day in late August, while waiting in the office of the inner city director, I noticed on his shelf a book titled *The Cross and the Switchblade* by David Wilkerson. Steve Clark had suggested we read that book, so I borrowed it and began reading it that night. I couldn't put it down until I had finished. It was a tremendous grace of the Lord. He was saying to me, "Ephphatha, John, be opened." Here was an incredible story of faith, pure gospel faith, in the slums of New York City where a young minister, armed with the Gospel and the power of the Holy Spirit, started a real Christian Renewal among the dregs of society.

In the ensuing months, I began to think that perhaps there was something in what Ralph and Steve had experienced and which they had related with so much enthusiasm back in March. I gave the book to others, particularly those who were working with me in the College Search for Maturity Program. Some were very interested in it; others disbelieved what they read. Wilkerson's story seemed too good to be true. To me and to a few others, it seemed so credible that we decided we would do as the Gospel says, "Come and see for yourself." In May 1968, we drove to Brooklyn, New York, about 175 miles from Providence, to visit Teen Challenge, a community mostly of former gang members and dope addicts, that Wilkerson had founded.

That Saturday was one of the most remarkable days of my life. The story was indeed true; in fact, it was more beautiful than portrayed in the book. I remember a former heroin addict showed us around that day. He was now a Christian apostle. Another worker had had over twenty-five trips on LSD. The spirit of community we found there amazed us. I was used to the community life of the College Seminary, but there were evident differences. After we had lunch with the young people, we helped with the dishes and noted the singing and laughing as they worked. Obviously, they were brothers who loved each other. It was real. In comparison, the community life at the seminary was rather routine. It was drab and lacked joy. I couldn't get over it! These joyful young Christians at Teen Challenge were former derelicts!

Later, they told us about the thirty-five centers they had founded in other cities around the country. With nothing but the belief in the power of the Gospel and the Holy Spirit, they had begun. And this was the most successful drug rehabilitation program in the country!

In addition to helping thousands kick habits, a number of the young former addicts and gang leaders were now very active for Christ. So many wanted to go into the ministry that they had to start their own Bible College to take care of the demand. The contrast with my experience was marked. We were having problems regarding vocations and we were working with the best of Christian young men.

That night Donald Wilkerson, David's brother, spoke at a rally about prayer. I had never heard anything like it. We were all moved, and at the end asked him, when the invitation came, to pray for us. Perhaps if this meeting had been in Providence, we might have been afraid to go forward and ask a Pentecostal minister to pray with us, but we were far enough away to feel free.

I remember Donald Wilkerson asking me, "What would you like me to pray for, Father?"

And I replied, "I work with college students and seminarians. I can use all the help I can get."

He prayed very beautifully, laying hands on my shoulder, and asking the Spirit to come in power, and fulfill that request, renewing my whole ministry. Nothing happened that moment, but somehow I believed in his prayer, and thanked him.

We left Brooklyn for lower Manhattan to visit the drop-in center, "The Lost Coin," in Greenwich Village. Young people with drug problems came in off the streets, were treated hospitably, and told about Christ in a simple direct way. We were profoundly impressed by the whole operation, and had much to discuss on the ride home.

THE EXPERIENCE: "and angels came and waited on him." Matt. 4:11

It was 4 a.m. when I arrived back in Providence and I remembered I had the eight and nine o'clock masses at St. Catherine's Church in Warwick. My main concern at the time was to get through them somehow, and then catch up on some rest. But the Lord had other and beautiful plans. Even now I can't explain it, but that eight o'clock mass was well, like brand new. Everything was ringing, singing— the words, the gestures, the people, especially God! I don't know what I said in the homily, but I could tell the people were really with me. As I walked off the altar, bewildered at what I'd experienced, only then did I remember Wilkerson praying over me the night before. Maybe, I thought, this was what was meant by the so-called "Baptism in the Spirit" experience. At the nine o'clock mass the unique experience was repeated as it has been at every mass since. I had always loved the mass and had experienced many powerful masses, especially at Cursillos and Searches, but I had never felt anything approaching what I felt that morning.

A couple of weeks later, the group that had visited Teen Challenge spent Pentecost weekend at a house in the country to seek the Spirit ourselves, and to read the Acts of the Apostles, hopefully to come to a greater fullness of the Spirit. We all agreed when that weekend at Escoheag was over, that it had been the richest we'd ever known. Profound peace settled upon that house, and upon each of us. Unfortunately, again there was little direct follow-up of that Pentecost weekend. Summer came. Once more I was involved with Cursillo and inner city work, training lay volunteers for community building. We talked a lot about getting together to pray, but actually did nothing about it.

Finally in September of 1968 I went to a weekend training retreat for high school leaders in the Search Program at Dominic Savig in Peacedale. I invited a few people who had been through the New York experience with me to help with that weekend. We talked to the retreatants about what had happened, first at Duquesne, about Pentecostal Renewal in the church, and about Teen Challenge. We tried to form a real sense of Christian Community with the young high school leaders.

We worked at it all day Saturday, and late Saturday night we met in the chapel to pray. As we prayed, we all felt that something was missing in our attempts to talk about Christian Community. All day we had examined every aspect of Christian Community, the psychological, the communitarian, and the philosophical. But something was missing; something wasn't clicking. In the silence we asked the Lord for guidance. And then a flash of thought, a grace, went through my mind. I had my New Testament in my hand and I said to myself, "You know, if you took just this little book and really tried to live it, believing what it says, and got a few others to do the same, maybe you'd have a real Christian Community." I was so struck by the thought, that I shared it with the others in the chapel. It was a grace, because it struck all of them the same way. We all said, "Yes, let's do that." Then it dawned on us that this was precisely what happened to Francis and his small band in the Middle Ages, and to Ignatius and his group in the 16th Century, real renewal from taking the Word of God seriously, not questioning it, just taking it and living by it.

I knew the Scripture pretty well, I thought. I had my Doctorate in Theology with a dissertation in Scripture. I belonged to the Catholic Biblical Association, and I had worked long and hard at exegeting texts, and getting to the various levels of Biblical criticism. But it was time to go beyond that and take the text for what it was, to live by it. We would see then what the Lord would do. I began to understand what the men of the Full Gospel Businessmen's Association mean by the title of their organization. Really living by the full Word of God can bring about true renewal, as we have subsequently seen.

The next day we shared with the young people on the retreat, and it caught on like fire! We gave each of them a copy of the New Testament. That weekend turned out to be a marvel! Several of the young people received the Baptism of the Holy Spirit experience and are today active in this movement in Providence and elsewhere.

About a month later, at the same retreat house, we had another Cursillo Leaders' Workshop. This time, I remember being eager to see Ralph Martin and Steve Clark again, to see if they had more to say about this movement. I was disappointed when they didn't appear on the program. There was, however, a remarkable man on the team, and everyone was strongly attracted by his talk. He didn't profess to belong to any Pentecostal Movement, but his message was ringing, very striking. At the end of the workshop I asked this man, Paul De Celles, Professor of Physics at Notre Dame, if he went to the Pentecostal prayer group at that college. He did.

That night I took him back to the seminary. It was located near the airport from which Paul was to fly back to Notre Dame the following morning. Far into the night Father Mort Smith, who was also on Cursillo Leaders' Workshop Team, and I listened to Paul. (Mort is now the Vice Chancellor for the Diocese of Newark.) But before we went into my room, I took Paul down to the shore of Narragansett Bay, and pointed out various places in the vicinity. Finally, I showed him Newport with its lights strung along the bridge in the distance. Paul commented, "That's where Terry Martin, Ralph Martin's younger sister, goes to school. You should look her up. She had some very interesting experiences at Ann Arbor this summer."

With that we went back to my room and Paul talked to us. About four a.m., just before breaking up to get a few hours sleep, Mort and I did a strange thing. We two priests knelt on the floor and asked Paul, a layman, to pray with us, to pray that we might experience some of the power he was talking about, and that we had seen in him. Very simply and very beautifully, he prayed over us. It was the first time we had ever heard a Catholic speak in tongues, pray in tongues. It was a very moving experience, although nothing very dramatic happened immediately. We just thanked him and believed, in faith, that his prayers were powerful.

I took Paul to the airport, taught classes all morning, and around noontime I sat at my desk, and picked up my breviary. The same remarkable thing happened with the breviary as had happened with mass at St. Catherine's some months before. The book was almost jumping in my hands. The psalms came alive as never before. The scripture had really begun to sing. With all my scriptural training, with all the time I had given to scripture reading, it was as if that was all nothing compared to this moment of grace. A light had been cast on them, and I learned more about the scripture in that moment than I did with all my years of study and training. And again I went back to Paul's praying over me, and the power of the Holy Spirit, and the idea of the Baptism in the Holy Spirit became very clear to me. That was what they meant by this experience of the Spirit lifting us up with new wisdom, new power, making the scriptures come alive, making the mass come alive. Here were the two poles of my priesthood, the Mass and the Scripture, now really alive. And they have remained very vivid to me ever since that moment, growing steadily more "living."

The following night was Tuesday, and I decided to phone Terry Martin. It is difficult to get a girl in a college dorm at ten o'clock at night, but I thought I'd give it a try. To my surprise, the phone was answered immediately. When I asked for Terry Martin, the voice replied, "This is Terry Martin."

I was even more astonished when she asked me, "Is this Father Randall?"

I had met Terry casually a year or so earlier through her brother Ralph but I had never phoned her, nor had I spoken to her in the interval. I was stunned when she recognized my voice. It seemed prophetic.

"Yes, how did you know?" I asked. "Did Paul tell you I was going to call?"

"Paul who?" questioned Terry.

"Paul De Celles," I said.

"Was he in town?"

19

Needless to say, I was intrigued, and arranged to see Terry the following Saturday at the seminary. (Later Terry told me that in August the Lord revealed to her that He would move in Rhode Island that year very strongly and use her. He specifically mentioned southern Rhode Island, western Rhode Island, and Providence. Terry returned to Salve Regina in the Fall and was waiting for the Lord to move, praying for it to begin. When I phoned she knew that was an answer.)

When Saturday came around, it was a big day at the seminary. Bishop McVinney was there celebrating mass for three hundred distinguished women of the Diocesan Council of Catholic Women. As I was concelebrating with several other priests, suddenly the chapel door opened and in came Terry, wearing a trench coat and dungarees and followed by five or six "hippies!" They looked like hippies in contrast to this distinguished gathering. Frankly, I wanted to fall through the floor. Everyone was surprised when the group walked up to Bishop McVinney at communion time, and very piously received from him. In the sacristy after mass, the Bishop asked the Rector, "Who were those young people?" The rector surmised they were friends of Father Tetreault who worked with young people in the city of Providence. I didn't say anything. I was just happy to make my escape.

The "hippies" were a group of young men from Ann Arbor who had decided, on the spur of the moment, to visit Terry that weekend. Now, as I look back, I realize it wasn't coincidence that they did so. That evening I gathered together all those from the seminary who might be interested and some people from outside who were working with me on the College Search Program. We gathered in the seminary library to listen to the young men. It was a strange experience—a really strange experience. Here were these "hippies" talking to us about Christ, about Faith, about what it meant to them. We were questioning them, whereas it might seem more appropriate the other way around. We were asking them, seminarians were asking, priests were asking, "Where did you get this kind of faith?" And they were telling us, remarkably well they were telling us, what faith meant to them. A spark was lit that night and I decided to follow it up.

A week or two later, I asked Terry if she would come back to speak to the seminarians about prayer. I was driving into Providence to pick her up that night and really wrestling with myself about whether or not I had made a terrible mistake. Here I was, an experienced spiritual director with education and training, going into Providence to pick up a nineteen year old girl to talk to the seminarians about prayer. Was I out of my mind? I wrestled with myself all the way in, until it finally dawned on me, and this was grace again, the Lord was saying, "Isn't it all grace?" And I had to say "yes." It was proven when Terry came to the seminary, and spoke ever so movingly about prayer. Something really was happening. Enough interest was generated now that five or six of us decided to meet weekly to pray, seeking the Spirit more fully in our lives.

In December 1968, a Cursillo Leaders' Retreat had been scheduled. I had been so moved by Terry and other young friends, especially Phil Thibodeau from Boston who had been at Ann Arbor also, that I asked the two of them if they would give the retreat with me to experienced Cursillo leaders from all over Rhode Island. It was taking a chance exposing these people to young college students, but I thought it was worth it. The retreat was remarkable; many received the Baptism, several of whom are still very active in the Pentecostal Movement in this area. One of those really touched by Terry that weekend was Sister Fran (Sr. Frances Maria Conway RSM), now a member of the Pastoral Team of our Word of God Community.

THE APPLICATION: "Thanks be to God, who through us is spreading the knowledge of Himself like a sweet smell everywhere." II Cor. 2:4

As of January 1969, a weekly prayer meeting was held every Sunday afternoon in the housing project apartment of Elliot Ryan, an inner city worker at Prospect Heights in nearby Pawtucket. At first we were only five or six, including Terry, for a month before she returned to Ann Arbor. But during those few short weeks she helped us to get used to praying in the Spirit. We were more and more intrigued. No one would miss a single meeting. Soon people began bringing friends. We phoned one another during the week, excitedly sharing what the Lord was teaching, what was happening in our lives. We began to pray together in twos and threes, in various places.

When Terry left in February we were concerned, but I remember her saying, "It's not my work. The Spirit will teach you and show you." We discovered this to be true, that it really was His work, because things continued growing after Terry left.

Time passed and by May we were about fifteen people meeting every week. A great desire rose in us to do more than just meet once a week on Sunday, the Lord's Day. We had a strong desire to form some kind of community and to have a community living experience that summer. The more we thought about it, the more we felt the Lord was drawing us to it.

Eleven of us were free and after praying a good deal, we were led to the Federal Hill section of Providence, to Holy Ghost Parish. Father Joseph, the pastor, had graciously invited us to come and work among his people, to try to create a spirit of prayer in the parish. I had met Father Joseph in the Cursillo Movement. We had the approval of the Bishop to experiment, and the Pastor's invitation, but we had nothing else. We had no money, no resources, except a firm conviction that the Lord was calling us, and a trust that if He wanted something done, He'd provide the means to do it.

With Father Joseph's help we were able to get a couple of apartments. One, over a barroom at 138 Knight Street, was where the girls would live. The men would be staying at an apartment across the street, and I would be living at the rectory. An example of how the Lord really blessed this undertaking concerned the two apartments we had rented for thirty-five dollars each. We took them, not knowing where we would get the money, but believing that we would have it in God's own time. The next day the landlord phoned the rectory and announced, "You know, Father, about those apartments I rented to you yesterday."

"Yes," I answered, not certain what it was I was supposed to know.

"You can have them" he continued, "rent free."

Well, that was the beginning of this kind of goodness in Providence. The Lord took care of us all that summer. We were often feeding twenty-five to thirty people a day and always had enough.

Another example of the kind of help the Lord gave us came a few weeks later when Russ Kirk, one of the young men who prayed with us every Sunday afternoon at Prospect Heights, arrived to pray one Friday. He was a college senior who had to work that summer to earn tuition money, even though he would have preferred to be with us. After praying that Friday morning, Russ was moved to wonder whether he should give up his job and come in faith to work with us, trusting that the Lord would provide the five hundred dollars he needed. He told us what he was thinking, and wanted our prayers and advice. We all thought, after praying about it, that he should step out in faith, risking the tuition money, and he agreed to do it. We had about two hundred dollars in the till, and we gave him that. Two days later, I was offering mass at the parish I helped at every Sunday. After mass, the pastor asked how things were going up in the city. He had not been that curious before, but I told him what was happening and that things were going very well. When he asked if we needed anything, I was about to say no, because I am proud. Instead, I said, "Well, we don't refuse anything."

He said, "Let me write you a check," and he gave it to me.

I was too embarrassed to open the check, and kept it folded until I reached my car. It was a check for three hundred dollars which we promptly gave to Russ when he came on Monday morning. Now he already had the five hundred dollars needed for tuition. The Lord did this for us. Time and time again that summer the Lord did similar things for us, and continues to pour out His blessings on what we are doing. We came to realize how literally true are the words of the Gospel, "Seek first the kingdom of heaven and everything else will be added to you."

That summer we took our program right out of the pages of *The Cross and the Switchblade*. After all, we thought, it had worked for them, why shouldn't it work for us? The program, basically, was to spend the whole morning in prayer, and, in the afternoon, to do as the Gospel says, to go out two by two into the neighborhood, telling everybody about Jesus Christ, about the Father's love for them, and in the evening, to invite people up to our apartments to talk, to pray, to listen to tapes by David Wilkerson, Nicky Cruz, and others telling the wonderful things of the Lord. And then we just let the Lord work very directly with His people.

It was a different approach for us, and at first we experienced difficulty adjusting to it. In inner city work in the past, we had tried to help the poor to organize the community into block clubs and the like. Others had taken poor children out on trips. Here, on Knight Street, we were going to talk directly about

Christ, nothing else. Our aim was something like St. Paul's going into Corinth, or Ephesus, or Philippi, and in our morning sessions of prayer, as we studied the Scripture carefully, we attempted to rediscover just how Paul preached the Word in those Greek cities. Every morning we went to mass at Holy Ghost Church, trying to put more life into it, rather than having our own liturgy. That way we were able to work in the context of the parish, and, also, to avoid appearing to be a separate underground church development. We decided to build up a parish prayer meeting. The first Sunday, Father Joseph spoke at all the masses urging people to come to this prayer experience. He told them about us and delivered a beautiful exhortation. That was the only time we ever really got a "plug," and it proved quasi-disastrous. The following evening was a disappointment; only about ten people showed up. We went ahead with the program just the same, trusting the Lord, praying, and trying to share our prayer experience with those who had come. The next week more came, fifteen maybe, and twenty came the week after. It just began to grow. Gospel was becoming Gospel, Good News, neighbor telling neighbor, and friend telling friend without any kind of public advertising.

By summer's end there were seventy people coming to the weekly prayer meeting.

Page after page of the Gospel came alive to us that summer. Another incident centered on the power of poverty. "Blessed are the poor, for theirs is the kingdom of Heaven." We arrived on Knight Street with nothing, and this endeared us to the neighborhood. People noticed we had little or no furniture, little or no food, and they began to come to us, these beautiful people of Federal Hill, bringing a spaghetti dinner, a table, a chair.

We were indebted to them, rather than indebting them to us in some patronizing way. As they brought good to us, food to us, they would ask us what we were doing there, and we told them very simply we had come to share the love of Christ.

Once, in front of a barroom, a group of men asked us the familiar question. We told them we wanted to share the love of God, our Father, with them, to share our knowledge of Jesus. One man said, very simply, and that was characteristic of everyone we met that summer, "Well, it's about time. We don't go to church, and so you come to us. Is that it?" We answered, "You've got it." Those men in front of the barroom proved to be our greatest friends even though, at first, I was tempted to think they might not be.

But on the first morning we were returning from mass at Holy Ghost when I saw two of the sisters, still in their habits, talking to the men in front of the barroom, I was horrified! It was providential that I was one hundred yards or so away, because in the interval it took me to reach them, the Lord had a chance to teach me. "Didn't I associate with publicans and sinners?" He asked. I realized that this was so. Instead of stopping the sisters from talking to the men for fear of what the Bishop might say, I went over and joined them. These men, as I have said, became our greatest friends and allies. They spread the word all over the Hill about what we were doing there. They came to see us themselves, prayed with us up on the third floor, and went out to spread the Good News.

Going out in the afternoon, two by two, seemed like a hard thing to us at first, but it proved to be easy. Adults were sitting on the doorsteps, there were kids at the city pool, and old men met for conversation and checkers in vest pocket parks. It was easy to mingle, to associate with them, especially empowered as we were by the prayer experience of the morning and led very directly by the Lord in amazing ways. After a week or two, we didn't go out any more in the afternoons because people were beginning to come to us morning, noon, and night. In fact, to allow time for prayer, we had to put a sign on the apartment door, "Please do not come in the morning." One after another, amazing things happened on the Hill that summer.

I remember in particular one striking incident. A girl, let's call her Ellie, who had been a pusher, came up one night. She told us later she had come to con us out of $80, but instead, she accepted Christ as her personal savior. When she finally left at two in the morning, she was filled with the Holy Spirit. She wanted to come every day, especially mornings, to pray with us, and she did. She was like the Samaritan woman in the Gospel, bringing the whole town to us. She especially wanted to bring a friend we'll call Joan, who had been a pusher like herself, and who was wanted by the police. Joan skipped a court appearance and an arrest warrant was out on her. Ellie said she was going to bring Joan up to the apartment that night, but night came and no Joan, no Ellie until eleven o'clock. Then Ellie arrived in tears. Joan had been arrested that night while having supper in a restaurant. Ellie had failed at one of her first ventures as an apostle and was not to be consoled.

I didn't know quite what to say to her, but that morning we had read in the Acts of the Apostles about Peter being in prison, and the whole Christian community praying for his release, which came about miraculously. I read the story to Ellie. I asked her, "Do you have that kind of faith? Jesus Christ is the same yesterday, today and forever! If we have that kind of faith, the same thing can happen today. Do you believe that?"

She whispered, "Yes." And then I asked, "Why don't we kneel down now and pray?" All the while, I was a bit bothered that Joan, unlike Peter, was not innocent. But we prayed anyhow. We prayed up a storm!

The next afternoon, I went out into the neighborhood as usual. Around five o'clock I came into the apartment for supper. I was surprised to see Ellie sitting at the kitchen table and Joan with her. Astonished, I asked what had happened, Joan explained, "Last night around eleven o'clock, in my jail cell, I don't know what happened, but, all of a sudden, I knew that I had God. I knew that God was with me. This morning I went before the judge, and I was released."

I was frequently astonished that summer as wonders happened over and over again. Joan told the Good News to her boyfriend down at the prison. She gave him copies of *The Cross and the Switchblade* and of the New Testament and the next thing we knew, we were going down to visit him and the fellow in the next cell. A jail apostolate was beginning. We had to abandon our prison apostolate at the end of the summer, but it was resumed by young men from Word of God and other communities, and very successfully. At one time, up to seventy men met for prayer each week.

Before summer's end the Lord led Sister Fran, Sue Reilly, and Irene Primeau, who gave up her teaching job to stay on, to take an apartment in the same area, which became the base of our operations. The last day of our summer apostolate, we felt we really had grown in the Lord, and were just waiting for Him to congratulate us. To our surprise, very clearly in prayer and prophecy, the Lord told us that we were still "babies on milk," and that He had protected us marvelously that summer. Now, He was going to lead us out into the desert and teach us, each in his own way. We didn't quite know what that meant; subsequently, we learned. As I look back on that experience, I don't think any of us fully believed in the existence of the devil or demons. Even though our work prospered that summer, and we had seen miracles, it was no thanks to us. We had been protected by the Lord that summer, without our awareness that He was, in fact, our shield.

As that winter approached, the numbers at the prayer meetings at Holy Ghost kept growing. In time the Lord led individual members and groups to split off and form communities in parishes, in cities, in towns, elsewhere around the state, and in our neighboring states. As a matter of fact, since that summer over thirty-five prayer groups have started in different areas of Rhode Island, and throughout New England, some of them now numbering over 400 members. When we look back on that summer, it seems incredible; we never intended any of this. All we intended, when we began, was that four or five of us get together every week, a little like a Cursillo reunion, and simply pray and seek the Spirit in depth. It was the Lord who was really building the city and doing it Himself, and supplying us with the power. To Him all the glory and all the credit, for we never intended any of this.

THE RENEWAL: "I will lead her out into the wilderness, and speak to her heart. From there I will give her the vineyards." Hosea 2

In June 1970, we must have numbered two hundred at the Holy Ghost prayer meeting. We really intended to resume the previous summer's operation, and were looking for a center hoping to start a library of books and tapes, where people could meet and learn more about the movement. But look as we did, we could find nothing. We prayed but nothing seemed to open up. We were discouraged but the Lord has His own ways and His own plans, and, finally, a totally unexpected invitation came to us. The Pieri family offered us their farm, out in the country at Little Compton. This certainly would not be inner city living, and I was tempted at first to reject the offer outright. But we said, "Let's pray about it and think about it." One night, while we were praying about the offer, and wondering whether we should accept the farm and use it for occasional retreats, the Lord seemed to tell us very clearly to get that farm. I remember the passage we received while praying about it. It was the beginning of John 6 when Jesus crossed the Sea of Galilee. Now the farm was across Narragansett Bay from Federal Hill. The Lord gave us great peace, and we knew He wanted us to go to Little Compton and so we did. Later we received passages like, "I shall lure you out into the wilderness to teach you," from Hosea, and the message was underlined in teachings from all parts of the Bible.

Still we had a burden about our Federal Hill apostolate and said, "What about the people on the Hill? What about the growth of the community?" It was as if the Lord answered, "Don't worry about it. I'll take care of it. I want you to go on a retreat; I want you to learn; I want you to grow; I want to form you Myself." And so we did. We went out into the country and thought. We taught ourselves, we taught each other, we listened, we prayed, and the Lord formed us in strength and depth. This was the Lord's tradition. John the Baptist and other servants of the Lord were led out into the desert and learned His way.

On weekends we invited the leadership of various other communities to the farm where they could share our experience of growth. These proved to be very fruitful weekends. The Lord did many marvelous things. Meanwhile, to our amazement, the prayer group on Federal Hill doubled that summer without our working in the area during the week.

People from Providence College summer school and others came in droves. It became ever more clear that this was the work of the Lord and not ours at all.

In the fall of 1970 the meetings continued to grow. Sister Fran, Sue Reilly, Irene Primeau, and Janice Luongo who had now joined them, moved from their apartment into another building. They found a home right next to Holy Ghost Church on Atwells Avenue, after months of prayer for a house. This building, subsequently, came to be called Philadelphia House, and was a center for people seeking the Lord in that area. It served for two years as a teaching center for members of the community and also as a coffee house.

Chapter II

"GO UP ONTO A HIGH MOUNTAIN" Isaiah 40:9

THE CALL: "Then He said to the priests: 'Take up the ark of the covenant, and cross at the head of the people.' " Joshua 3:6

In the spring of 1971 things had grown so busy with the development of the prayer community and my work at the seminary that it was impossible to continue both commitments. The telephone was ringing, people were writing letters and coming to see me at all hours. I began to think very seriously about choosing between the prayer community or the seminary.

Around the same time Father Raymond Kelly, Librarian at Our Lady of Providence Seminary, and a colleague of mine, became very interested in the prayer movement and I shared the experience with him. He was due to become a pastor within two years and thought that the prayer movement would be the best hope of revitalizing a parish. The more we shared and prayed, the more we seemed led to enter into parish work together.

We knew that the Charismatic Renewal, if it ever were going to prove itself, would have to show what it could do in transforming a parish, a territorial parish, an ordinary parish. We were led to propose to the Bishop that we be given an opportunity to try this approach in running a parish, not just having a once-a-week prayer meeting, but building a whole parish around this concept. To our surprise Bishop McVinney and the Diocesan Personnel Board accepted the idea almost immediately. Shortly thereafter Father Kelly was named pastor of St. Patrick's Parish in Providence, and I was his assistant.

A very beautiful story needs to be told here. One year previously when we were looking for a center of operation for the summer of 1970 (and went, eventually, to the farm in Little Compton), Carol Melucci prayed one day about a center and had a vision prophecy in which she saw the name State Street on a street sign and a large house on a corner. I knew where State Street was, although Carol didn't, not being a Providence resident. There was a convent there which the Sisters of Mercy were permanently vacating that summer due to the closing of St. Patrick's parish school. I went to Bishop McVinney and asked

41

him if we could use that convent. The Bishop sent me to the Pastor, who promised he would put our request before the parish. Other groups were seeking the building too, and subsequently the convent was awarded to one of them. One year later, to our surprise, the Bishop handed Father Kelly and me St. Patrick's Parish, not only the old convent, but the whole parish plant. The ways of the Lord are truly marvelous!

THE CROSSING: "When you see the ark of the covenant of Yahweh your God and the levitical priests carrying it, you must leave the place where you are standing and follow the ark." Joshua 3:3.

In July 1971, Father Kelly and I were in St. Patrick's Parish on Smith Hill. The prayer group, now about 500 people, was across the Canal at Holy Ghost Parish in Federal Hill. We were not decided on whether we should move the prayer group over to St. Patrick's. Perhaps it would be best, we thought, to start anew at St. Patrick's, leaving the original group at Holy Ghost to continue revitalizing things there and throughout the state. It would be easier initially if we didn't have to bring a big group into our new parish where we knew nobody. So we left the prayer group at Holy Ghost. But then, one day in August, our pastoral team (at the time Sister Fran, Matt Tierney and I), while at prayer, was clearly told by the Lord that He wanted the whole prayer group brought to St. Patrick's. He wanted to use the resources of this group to help revitalize the parish community. The scripture passage that most impressed us was from I Samuel 6, the moving of the ark of the covenant from one town to another. We were convinced then that the Lord wanted us to move the whole group, so we took the risk of doing it.

When I went to tell the Pastor of Holy Ghost about our determination to move, we didn't know how he would react. Father Joseph had been so good to us, so hospitable, we would truly grieve if we offended him. He met us and even before we said a word, told us that he thought it best we move because he didn't have the resources to handle the growing crowds. So we moved the prayer group from Holy Ghost to St. Patrick's.

Father Kelly hadn't yet received the Baptism in the Holy Spirit experience, but he was very willing and open to the whole movement. Sr. Fran gave him the Life in the Spirit Seminars, and Ray grew very beautifully through it all, soon becoming a member of our pastoral team, filled with the Spirit and one of our really great leaders.

The old convent on the corner of State Street soon became a great center of our operation. Twelve girls, some sisters, some laywomen, decided they really wanted to live in Christian Community in the old convent. Sister Fran and Irene Primeau left Philadelphia House to become part of the original group on State Street. One weekend on retreat, the group prayed about the house, and heard the Lord name it for them. He called it the House of Faith, a name which has proved itself so remarkably ever since. A beautiful Christian Community began to form around the House of Faith, between the rectory and the House of Faith especially, but also open to all the community and the parish. We would all meet at 9 a.m. prayer at the House of Faith, priests, sisters, lay people. We would have lunch at the rectory together, and supper together at the House of Faith. A nucleus of Christian community was forming. Seminars were taught in the House of Faith; morning prayer was open to all the community members, and some came every morning; counseling, auditing tapes, deliverances, all were carried on there. Few community members have not had a deep experience there.

After familiarizing ourselves with the parish, we knew what we strongly suspected: many problems existed there. The parish was situated in a declining neighborhood. The freeway had split it in two, isolating the church, the rectory, and the convent on the east side of Interstate 95, while virtually all the parish that remained after the highway construction had wiped away house after house, was on the west. The parish school had closed the previous year. Many parishioners were convinced, in short, that Father Kelly and I had really come to bury the parish, just as its neighbor parish, Immaculate Conception had died a few years earlier with urban redevelopment. In fact, rumor was strong that the Church property had already been earmarked by the state for growth of its plant; the State House was right across the street. State office buildings ringed us to the west, the north and the south. In addition, the parish was reduced to less than half its former size and was in debt (which explained the closing of the school). This, incidentally, did not dismay Father Kelly or me. We were happy the school was closed because, at this point, we didn't believe particularly in parochial education with all the problems it brought. We believed that Christ never taught groups of children, alone. This is something to really think about. He taught just adults. He didn't even teach groups of teenagers. We were determined that we would concentrate our efforts on an adult community.

We had been told by the previous parish administration that it would be a relatively easy task to lease the school building which we would have to do to solve financial problems. The city was interested in renting it and so was the state. We waited, anticipating action on the school, but nothing happened. September went by, and so did October, November, and December with debts mounting and no leasing of the school.

Meantime, most of the people in the parish were taking quite well the fact that a large prayer meeting was held in the church basement every Thursday night. Father Kelly and I were trying to serve both communities, the prayer community, and the parish community, an all-absorbing task.

THE SHEPHERD: "I mean to raise up a shepherd, my servant David, and to put him in charge of them, and he will pasture them and be their shepherd." Ezekiel 34:23

In January 1972, at the Annual Ann Arbor Conference for Leaders, from which we had always received so much benefit for the growth of our community, some remarkable events occurred. We met some members of the Church of the Redeemer, Episcopal, in Houston, Texas, among whom was Jerry Barker who had just written an article appearing in the December issue of the magazine *New Covenant*. We knew that Redeemer Parish was in an inner city changing neighborhood, and was very much like St. Patrick's in population shift and decline, and financial adversity. We were very interested in talking to Jerry, and told him our situation at St. Patrick's with a large prayer group and a traditional parish attempting to merge. Jerry made one very pertinent observation. In his opinion, we really had not one parish but two. I was the pastor of one, the Word of God Community, and Ray Kelly was the pastor of St. Patrick's Parish. It could be fatal, Jerry said, if we didn't join the two under one leadership. He spoke about how God worked in the

Bible this way, about the Moses concept of leading God's people.

The Moses reference really rang home because at a prayer meeting two or three months previously, we had a very, very strong prophecy about God's raising up a new Moses to lead His people in Providence. So we returned to Providence and told Ray Kelly and the other leaders of our prayer community what Jerry had said. Most responded beautifully. Father Kelly, who was already Pastor of St. Patrick's Parish, and a member of the Pastoral Team of the Word of God Community (which had now been expanded to include Ray McMahon, a married layman), now became our new Moses. The parish and the prayer community would become one under his leadership. The Lord has anointed Ray Kelly as a gifted shepherd, and we see how this really is God's plan that the resources of the prayer community are, in God's Providence, to be put at the disposal of building up St. Patrick's parish.

When spring came, the newly consecrated Bishop of Providence, Louis B. Gelineau (who has proved to be friendly to our whole movement and is a real grace of God to us), appointed Father Kelly Director of Charismatic

Renewal in the Diocese. Leaders from other Charismatic groups had already been meeting monthly with the leadership of Word of God Community for sharing, prayer and planning. The aim was to coordinate and develop the one body of Christ across all these groups, and to give the renewal common leadership, since leadership is so important to the development of the Charismatic Renewal. In addition, we have planned days of renewal, four times a year, sponsored by all the communities. As the Pastor of the Word of God Community, Ray Kelly had experienced fellowship with the very people he was called to represent in the chancery.

THE GARDEN: "But Jesus called the children to him and said, 'Let the little children come to me, and do not stop them; for it is to such as these that the kingdom of God belongs.' "
Luke 18:16

A sudden offer came in God's Providence and really showed His plan, because it was nothing we would ever have considered. Right after we had made Ray the pastor of both communities, merging the Word of God Community with St. Patrick's Parish, an offer came for a local college to buy the vacant school building for $350,000. It was a very tempting offer indeed! The problem was that if the school was sold, it would mean the loss of the property to the parish. Then, if the state were to take over the parish plant, it would mean there would be no place for expansion and result in the eventual and probable death of St. Patrick's Parish. The school building was the only parish property west of the Interstate highway, and so we were very slow to accept that offer. We had about a week to think and pray about it — which we did.

During that week the Lord put the seed of this idea in one of us: "Why don't you reopen the school?" The idea seemed preposterous to us at first but the more it was enunciated, the more people were struck by it. We suddenly discovered that with the large prayer group, we had the resources to possibly reopen the school. The idea of a school where Jesus could really be Lord, where children from the earliest ages could be exposed and open to the working of the Holy Spirit excited people. When we brought this idea to the community, it gained ready acceptance. The following Sunday we were able to bring this news of a possible reopening of the school to the people at the Sunday masses, announcing that we were going to have a parish meeting to discuss this subject. It proved to be a bombshell of an announcement letting people in the parish know that perhaps this prayer community could offer something besides a weekly prayer meeting with all the "emotionalism," excitement and crowds. Perhaps the prayer community could do something really constructive in the rebuilding of St. Patrick's Parish, namely and specifically, reopening the school. We explained to the people that if we were to reopen the school, it would be under very specific grounds; that we really did believe principally in educating adults and that we wanted this to be an adult or family-centered school. We would only admit to this school children of parents who were willing to go through an eight week Life in the Spirit Seminar so that they could be exposed to what the children would receive.

Many parents readily accepted this idea and were enthusiastic, to our pleasant surprise, about the whole undertaking. What God was marvelously doing here was bringing together two communities, the parish community and the Word of God Community, a very difficult undertaking. Anyone who has any experience with the Charismatic Movement in a parish knows how it can divide instead of unite. But now, through this school, which we never intended to reopen ourselves, God was answering a great need the parish had felt, a great want, namely their school, and at the same time remarkably gaining the acceptance and the excitement of the people in the Word of God Community.

And so the school was launched. Parents, many parents, went through the seminars on Sunday mornings after the ten o'clock mass, and on Tuesday nights, and began to become part of the weekly prayer meeting. A beautiful mingling of people from outside and inside the parish began. In fact, the preparing of the school for operation in the summer of 1972 was an amazing community building operation in itself. Men from all over Providence began laying new floors, painting the walls, putting in new driveways, preparing the grounds. Men, women, and children were doing this on Saturday afternoons and on week day evenings. As people worked to ready the school, a sense of community bloomed.

During the 1972-1973 school year more than two hundred children from all parts of the city and environs attended our school. Some travelled an hour each way. Community members came to teach, to aid teachers, to work in the office or on the playground. Some came full time, some part time. Some received no salary, others a stipend. During the summer of 1973 a few community members were deeply engaged in research, curriculum planning, refining next year's program. We are not committed to any one approach, but we know God wants this school, and He wants it to be a superb school.

THE VINEYARD: "I gave you a land, where you never toiled, you live in towns you never built; you eat now from vineyards and olive groves you never planted." Joshua 24:13

By the Spring of 1972 we had developed an interesting problem. Our Thursday night prayer meeting, which had grown to six or seven hundred at this time, was difficult in the sense that it had a double focus. There was a constant stream of new people, as well as the large group who had been coming to the prayer meeting for years and had already developed to varying degrees of maturity. A dilemma was facing us. Do you give new teaching or advanced teaching to this mixed group? We were led to resolve the problem by splitting the group in two, and having an evening specifically devoted to new people on Friday night which we would call our Renewal Center Operation. The Life in the Spirit Seminar would be our main focus after the meetings. We would invite people who had finished the Life in the Spirit Seminars and who wanted to commit themselves to a service in St. Patrick's Parish Community, to devote themselves to the building up of St. Patrick's Parish, to come on Wednesday nights, at which time we would have a prayer meeting and Mass together. This proved to be a very fruitful move. Subsequently, the Lord led us to devote that meeting entirely to scripture study and teaching, our main liturgy now being the 10:00 Mass on Sunday. The Friday night prayer meeting was cut down to three or four hundred at first, but it is growing back up to around 700, and the Wednesday night community is now around 300.

In June 1972, Reverend Graham Pulkingham, from the Church of the Redeemer in Houston, Texas came to Rhode Island at the invitation of Episcopal ministers. Father Graham met privately with the Pastoral Team and with a group of leaders from Word of God and other communities the second weekend in June. As Graham talked about the Church of the Redeemer, we were again aware of the parallels between his parish and ours, as we were when we talked with Jerry Barker in Ann Arbor. But we heard Graham talk about a total commitment, a laying down of life, goods, privacy, self for the Body of Christ. He told us about households that were living the Acts of the Apostles. Many of our people were already led by the Lord to sell their homes in other parts of Providence, and in the surrounding suburbs, and to move into or back into St. Patrick's parish. But Graham's message gave a deeper meaning to living in a parish. The message of the Christian household was the Lord's word to us.

It was a message our people quickly took to heart, and many extended family households have been formed, with the advice and guidance of the Pastoral Team. At present there are more than fifteen homes open to whomever the Lord sends, either as a guest, or as a permanent member of the household family.

Something which had burdened us for months had to be dealt with immediately in September 1972, although it caused us and would cause the people of St. Patrick's great pain. The beautiful old church which had been a city landmark since 1910, standing on a height opposite the Capitol of the State of Rhode Island, was in imminent danger of falling down. We had long been aware of cracks and fissures in the brick facade, but, after a hurricane, bits of mortar and pieces of moulding plummeted from the high walls. Whenever there were strong winds, the east wall could be seen to sway.

Father Kelly called the Diocesan Building Inspector who examined the structure and ordered the building closed within two weeks. We roped off the right side of the nave immediately, that wall appearing most in danger of falling. We learned from the building inspector that faulty original construction had failed to bond the brick facade to the inner wall of the church. So, in fact, the outer wall could collapse outwardly onto the streets and pavements below, or the inner wall could collapse showering stone and mortar into the pews, perhaps causing great disaster if the church were occupied.

We explored every possibility which might lead to the saving of the building, and learned that three quarters of a million dollars would be needed to reinforce the walls, without any guarantee that this would be more than very temporary. In the past decades, thousands of dollars had been poured into reinforcement, and we found ourselves facing the structural defects once again. Father Kelly, the trustees, and I concluded that as far as reinforcement was concerned, we couldn't afford it, and it wouldn't work.

A parish meeting was held, at which representatives of the Diocesan Building Office and the Chancery explained the problem, and the inability of the diocese to extend funds for the church at this time. Many questions were asked of them and of Father Kelly. The people of the parish revealed their love for the church, and their grief that the building was to be abandoned. They sought and received our assurance that every effort would be made to remove and preserve the stained glass windows, the paintings and other art work.

At this meeting, in the news media and at subsequent Sunday masses, Father Kelly and I answered the basic cry, "Please don't kill the parish. Don't let it die." We assured the people that a building was not the parish, but rather, the people were the church, and the life of the parish was within them. Father Kelly and I openly committed ourselves, our lives, to St. Patrick's Parish and its people. This was a permanent commitment on our part, not, in any sense, a temporary assignment. The Lord had sent us, not to bury the parish, but to raise up the parish, and with God's help we would not let the parish die. I felt moved to reveal to the parishioners that I expected, at any time, that I would be offered a parish of my own, and when the offer came that I would refuse it. I would remain Assistant Pastor of St. Patrick's rather than become Pastor in a parish of my own because

I fully believed that St. Patrick's was my parish, the one the Lord led me to with Father Kelly a year earlier. Unless the Lord led me out, I would never leave it.

Well, the parish didn't die. God is faithful! We had to make some accommodations, of course. All services had to move into the school. It was the hand of the Lord that stopped its sale a year earlier and led us to preserve it, though we truly needed the money it would have brought, and it was the hand of the Lord that led us to renovate it and open the school that September, though we originally had no desire to do that.

Once again we saw Gospel was becoming Gospel. The message of Romans 8:28, "We know that God makes all things work together for the good of those who have been called according to his decree," was real; we were living it now. The parish moved into the school for mass, for baptisms, for confession, for vigils, for goal planning sessions. The community was in the school for Wednesday and Friday night prayer meetings, for Tuesday and Sunday night Foundations Courses, for parties, and reunions, for meetings and meditation. The two groups met head on, looked each other over, decided they found each other interesting, began to mingle more, and are fast becoming one. The ways of the Lord are amazing!

In November 1972, a day of renewal was planned for all Charismatic Christians in Rhode Island, and the speaker was Graham Pulkingham of the Church of the Redeemer in Houston. The message that day at Barrington College was to honor one's primary commitment, living according to the responsibilities it placed on one, and to seek Christ in your brother. This meeting and subsequent private meetings between Graham and the Pastoral Team, led us to invite The Fishermen to Providence. The Fishermen, a group of young evangelists from Redeemer Parish, lived with us in two households for seven weeks in the beginning of 1973. They shared their kind of community living with us and made many loving friends. As a matter of fact, when they left for New York to board a plane bound for Coventry, England, four car loads of us drove down with them to see them off. That was a round trip of 375 miles, but we did it gladly to extend our time with them.

Another occasion that brought the parish and the community together and gave each an opportunity to treat the other with love, came at St. Patrick's Parish Reunion on May 4, 1973. Father Jude McGeough, S.S.C., who had joined us at the rectory in the summer of 1972 and become part of the Pastoral Team in January 1973, headed up a group of parishioners and community members who planned the dinner dance, and prepared an excellent book, richly illustrated, containing a history of the parish. About 1200 parishioners, former parishioners who had moved out of the neighborhood, and community members who were moving in, or working in the parish, met to celebrate the health and longevity of St. Patrick's.

Early in 1973, at the direction of Bishop Gelineau, all the parishes in the diocese met first in deaneries and subsequently, in individual parish groups for "goal setting." Each parish was expected to determine its general long range objectives, and more specific goals the parish hoped to achieve in the next five years.

At St. Patrick's our "goal setting" committee included a representation of the parishioners, some of whom were members of the Word of God Community, and the Pastoral Team.

Now it was vitally important that the parish

and the community share the same vision. The goals decided upon, and to which we would pledge our resources in time, in money, and in work, would have to be supportable by all. With this in mind some of us fasted for two days prior to the first parish meeting. The day, I remember, had been full of minor disasters and we went to the meeting tired and somewhat apprehensive. As parish and community matters were shared openly including financial resources, preferences regarding music and liturgy, attitudes toward the school, prayer meetings, and many other areas, we knew that one vision could be shared by us all. One of the first goals some of the parishioners wanted to achieve was that the parish and the community would he one.

After the meeting, we received a phone call from Virginia. Betty Hayes, formerly from Providence, and now living in the South, had felt moved to pray for us that day. Even though it was late she called to share the prophecy the Lord gave her about us, "Your enemies are now as the footstool at your feet." She asked us if that made any sense, and we assured her that Satan, the enemy, had been at work that day in our midst, but that the Lord had triumphed that very evening.

In June 1973, the St. Patrick's Goal Setting Committee presented Bishop Gelineau with the following goals:

1. To put the parish on such a basis that it will be financially sound, i.e., operating on a budget which not only will take care of current operational needs, but also allow for replacement, capital improvements, and the development of programs.

2. To have a church building in which to worship.

3. To have fifty men and women involved in leadership roles in the parish.

4. To have sixty percent of those associated with St. Patrick's Parish by record involved in some activity in the parish.

5. That organized and coordinated activities be established in which thirty percent of the youth of the area between the ages of ten and seventeen would participate.

Census studies indicated the number of elderly people in Smith Hill was large and increasing. We established a ministry to visit the sick and shut-ins which uncovered so much loneliness, so much need, even though we had only begun to scratch the surface.

On Thanksgiving Day 1972 we hosted a turkey dinner for over three hundred residents of Smith Hill. A whole crowd of the community members ran cars all over the Hill the whole afternoon picking up and dropping off so many who would have eaten alone, or perhaps not at all. Dancing and singing followed the meal where people of all ages, children and adults, came together to thank God for His love and to break bread with each other. It is interesting to note that some who came wanted to make a donation for the dinner. They were not destitute but they needed friends.

As December drew on we determined to have a dinner on Christmas Day. At first we wondered if our people would be able to give up the day to serve the meal, to chauffeur, to entertain our brothers and sisters who might be alone. Christmas arrived and whole families came to work, some bringing relatives from other states. We had plenty of help and many of our people made new friends sitting at the long paper covered tables in the auditorium. More than two hundred and fifty people came, and the singing went on for hours.

When we established participation by sixty percent of the parishioners in some parish activity as one of our goals, we had a special desire to include the retired members of the community. Carroll Tower, a high rise apartment for the elderly, opened in June 1973 across Smith Street from the school. We planned to visit, surveying the interests of the people and inviting them to parish activities. We have begun doing that and are also celebrating mass there each month. Some of our neighbors at Carroll Tower come to prayer meetings, and more come to mass daily or on Sunday. On August 9, 1973, we sponsored a Welcome Party at the Tower which was attended by almost all the one hundred fifty residents. Father Jude organized a committee restricted to people over sixty. They planned a catered supper and a concert by The Word of God Singers. When we learned that some of the Jewish residents expected to arrive after the supper because they observed the dietary laws, we arranged for a special kosher table catered by a local delicatessen.

After the supper and concert the guests

were invited to a dance with music by some of our young people. They were afraid, at first, because they didn't know the kind of music the residents preferred for dancing. And then Ann Toye, who had played piano at St. Patrick's Minstrel Shows for years, took the lead at the piano. For three hours Ann played, taking only a brief intermission when she broke a finger nail, coming back bandaged but smiling to play on until eleven o'clock with the bass, the guitar, the drums, and the flute accompanying.

The party was only a beginning, of course. We continue to visit, and now as we come and go many of the Carroll Tower residents wave, call greetings and respond to the fact that we are happy that God called them to live on Smith Street across from our school.

The Lord has poured out His goodness on us through many of our brothers and sisters. We had a need for a place in the country where our ministries or small groups of our people could go to make a weekend retreat of prayer and sharing. The retreat houses in the area were too expensive, too difficult to book, or too small. And so we had a need. Into this need stepped Louise Pastille, a long time member of our community. She and her husband had planned and had construction started on a house in Connecticut, just over the border of Rhode Island. It was set on a wooded piece of property with a pond and many brooks nearby, a lovely, lonely place. Then Dr. Pastille died, and Louise did not think she would ever finish the house. But the Lord led her to do so, and beautifully, too, and to give the house to us for retreats any weekend, or week day we want to use it. Louise received the name Zion for the house when she prayed to the Lord about it, and it is well named. Many miracles have been worked in Zion; there is a retreat there almost every weekend; hearts have been changed, spiritual gifts have been poured out, blessings have abounded in Zion.

In September 1972 when our school opened, seven of the women who would be working in it, both religious and lay women, had no place to live together until their house on Washburn Street was renovated. Mary McLaughlin, another long time community member, was living alone after the recent death of her father. Mary invited the faculty members mentioned to share her home on Claremont Street. In the course of the year, Mary was moved by the Lord to sell her house, to assume ownership of the house on

Washburn Street, and to put her savings into renovating it and providing every comfort. Mary died on July 12, 1973, only days before the move to Washburn Street was scheduled. One community member observed that Mary's parting was a sure sign that we were coming of age as a community. "When the Lord removes a piece of the strong backbone of our community, it must mean He knows we are strong enough to stand without it." We celebrated with a sad joy at Mary's funeral mass, knowing that she has entered another stage in the community of saints. We agreed with one of Mary's favorite thoughts on death, "Death is not darkness. It is turning down the lamp, when dawn has broken."

These generous friends are only a few of so very, very many. The Lord blesses us in so many ways. May His name be praised forever!

Chapter III
TRUST IN PROVIDENCE:
Psalm 127

> *If Yahweh does not build the house,*
>   *in vain the masons toil;*
> *If Yahweh does not guard the city,*
>   *in vain the sentries watch.*
>
> *In vain you get up earlier,*
>   *and put off going to bed,*
>   *sweating to make a living,*
> *Since he provides for his beloved*
>   *as they sleep.*
>   PSALM 127:1-2.

Where do we go from here? What does the Lord intend for us in the future? God only knows! Everything, thus far, has been a surprise; nothing was planned. Out of prayer the Lord just led us from one step to another. It has been the most exciting six years that one could possibly imagine. He's given us visions of what is to come after we get St. Patrick's Parish more organized. He has just shown us that He wants to do fantastic work in renewing the whole Church in the area, and in the world, and that He plans to use us very powerfully in this kind of development. Day by day we receive invitations to go to various parishes and CCD groups, ministers' gatherings, priests' gatherings, locally in New England, and throughout the nation. Presently we have to turn down most of these offers because the Lord wants us to concentrate on building up the St. Patrick's Parish Community that it might be a city on the mountain, a light that can't be hidden, a parish that's come alive through the Charismatic Renewal, giving hope to other parishes that it can be done, not by men, not even by the joint efforts of men, but by God Who gives the growth in all circumstances. Unless the Lord builds the city, they labor in vain who build it.

One of the fruits of Vatican II was a rebirth of the mystery of Pentecost in this world. Pope John XXIII prayed that there might be a new Pentecost in our times. We saw it begin to flower at Vatican II. But that was just a beginning. The Catholic Charismatic Renewal in this country, along with the Pentecostal Movement and the Neo-Pentecostal Movement, are simple evidence of what the Lord really wants to do in our times, namely to bring the power of His Spirit back into full play.

What is really happening, I think, is akin to

what happened in the 50's and 60's with the rediscovery of the centrality of Easter in our lives. The Pascal Mystery, discovered in books like Durwell's *The Resurrection*, having an effect back in the 50's and 60's is finally flowering into our new Mass for Christian Burial, and the joy in our church, and all the joy in our Christianity today, centering around Easter.

From time to time in the church, different mysteries seem to get overlooked and passed over, not given the importance they deserve. Thus, the mystery of Easter was some time ago. Now, it seems to me that what the Lord is doing in our times is to underline and emphasize the mystery of Pentecost once again, not just to raise up in the Church a Pentecostal Movement, another group alongside many other groups in renewing the church, or even a Charismatic Renewal. Pentecostal movement, yes. Charismatic Renewal, yes, but much more than that. What the Lord really wants to do is bring the importance of the Holy Spirit to the whole Church in order to renew every aspect of Church life. We see fantastic implications for the Liturgical Movement, for the Biblical Movement, for the Ecumenical Movement, and for Social Action, once vitalized by the works of the Holy Spirit and the power of the Holy Spirit. Imagine the results in human relations, in communities, between nations, among peoples everywhere. We are just beginning to see what He's doing in His Church and it's amazing!

If we were to give a title to the kind of thing the Lord is doing in His Church, or the kind of movement that's happening, it wouldn't be Pentecostal Movement, it wouldn't be Charismatic Renewal, because they are only part of the whole thing, just as Christmas is part of the whole message, Easter is part of the message, Pentecost is part of the message, but not the whole message. There is something more to it than that. We call ourselves by the title "Word of God Community" to denote our commitment to living by the whole Word of God—getting back to the Word of God and living by it.

We used to say at mass, "Formed by the Word of God, we dare to say, Our Father." Pope Paul, at the end of one of the sessions of Vatican II, gathered all the Protestant observers together and gave each a gold bound copy of the New Testament and said to them all, "Gentlemen, let's all go home and read this book because in it, one day, I believe we will find our unity." This Paul really believes.

In the Word of God come alive, and in the inspiration of the Holy Spirit, we are going to see God renew His whole church, every aspect of it. The mystery of Pentecost, along with the mystery of Easter, is going to bring about renewal in our times which we have never seen equalled in history. As we say in one of the Eucharistic Canons, "We thank You, Lord, for letting us stand in Your Presence and serve You;" or again in the liturgy, "To know You, Lord, is to live; to serve you is to reign." It is God who builds His church, and the dignity and honor of man is to serve Him, to serve Him using His power and His wisdom.

It seems to me that in the Church today, many people who have tried genuine renewal following Vatican II are running out of gas, out of steam, because they have tried to do it with their own effort. They are working from early morning to late at night, as Psalm 127 says, and getting very tired in the process; many are becoming disillusioned and embittered. Perhaps that has to happen. Perhaps that has to happen until we learn that the power, the wisdom, the kingdom and the glory is the Lord's. "The kingship is the Lord's," as the end of the book of Obadiah says. Jesus is Lord. Jesus is the same yesterday, today and forever. What's really happening is that Jesus is building up the kingdom of His Father right in our midst. He's still here in power working miracles, speaking prophetically, giving out wisdom. All we have to do is seek Him, seek Him deeply and He will transform us, and transform our parishes into living parishes, our communities into living communities. What God the Father wants to do in our time is to build up in every city and every town a Body of His Son, a whole Body, where people can come and see Jesus Christ, feel His healing power, see His wisdom, hear His inspired preaching, reach out and touch Him, just as the crowd of Galilee did. This is what's happening. This is total renewal of His Church by God Himself.

Praise Him!

OF RELATED INTEREST

ATTAINING SPIRITUAL MATURITY
FOR CONTEMPLATION
(According to St. John of the Cross)

- For charismatic and traditional Christians
- For mature religious in active or contemplative institutes
- For sisters in Formation, seminarians, brothers
- For retreatants, students, members of prayer groups

By Venard Poolusney, O. Carm.
An invaluable introduction to all that the Mystical Doctor teaches those setting out on the ultimate spiritual journey. Many enthusiastically reach for the works of St. John soon after taking first steps toward the riches of deeper prayer, only to become discouraged without a "key" to unlock the treasure within. Father Venard, whose *Union with the Lord in Prayer* is so successful, now provides a compact bridge across the centuries and the specifically Carmelite terminology to the heart of the spiritual life — LOVE.

Among the topics examined are: the desire for perfection . . . self knowledge . . . knowledge of God . . . sensible consolations . . . the presence of God . . . faults of beginners . . . spiritual sins (such as pride, avarice, envy, gluttony, etc.) . . . detachment (mortification) . . . trials and temptations . . . practice of virtues and good works . . . and the passive night of the senses.

Special advice is included for those in the Charismatic Renewal, who through their Baptism in the Spirit have been given an experience of the presence of God. $.85.

Some comments on ATTAINING SPIRITUAL MATURITY FOR CONTEMPLATION.

"At long last an incentive to a more profound study of St. John of the Cross. This will be welcomed by all who wish an unerring guide in the spiritual life." — Sister Roseanne

"An invaluable aid. It helps one to understand the hindrances and pitfalls on the way. Practical—concise —illuminating!"—Dundee Borrelli (5 year Charismatic)

"This excellent book has synthesized the writings of the Great Doctor of the Church concerning beginners in the Spiritual Life. The author's approach is very easy to understand and can well be used as a syllabus for those instructing in Formation."—Rev. Sister Diane —Novice Mistress

"I always hoped that someone would do this! Praise the Lord!" —Rev. Sister Marice Dominica

"Father Venard has done a great service to those interested in a real union with God. In this book Father makes St. John come across as his real self: Doctor, teacher, and possessor of Divine Love, leading one to desire to read his complete works. The examples are easily understood and appreciated. Apropos to our times, Father V. co-relates the experience in the Charismatic Renewal to the experience of God in contemplative prayer. He also makes quite plain that love is the beginning, love is the way, love is the end, and he encourages all who seek God to do so perseveringly; that this Spiritual Perfection is for all!"—Rev. Sister Mary Dolores, O.P.—Reverend Mother Superior

"As a Charismatic, I found guidelines for my soul, yet the freedom to let the Spirit grow. Yes, even the dark night is good."—Joyce Warren

"This direction to contemplative prayer is brought to us with simplicity and clearness."—Rev. Sister Camillus

UNION WITH THE LORD IN PRAYER
Beyond Meditation To Affective Prayer
Aspiration and Contemplation

By Venard Poslusney, O. Carm. This practical guidebook to deeper prayer is meeting with resounding success. Published less than a year, it is nearing a third large printing. Before *Union with the Lord in Prayer*, many looked vainly for brief, loving help in reaching their spiritual goal—the goal set this year *for all Christians* by the U. S. Bishops. In their statement of fundamental doctrine they declared: "*All Christians* should learn to be gradually led on by more mature prayer—to meditation, contemplation, and union with God."

A few of the important topics in this first book by the noted Carmelite retreat master and spiritual article writer are:

- Meditation—only a first "step" to deeper prayer
- Affective Prayer—when words become unnecessary
- Prayer of Simplicity—the soul is absorbed in silent sweet love of the Lord

Concrete help is clearly given in essential areas such as: when to change from meditation to affective prayer . . . the various kinds of affection . . . model aspirations . . . the practice of the presence of God . . . and, when to change from affective prayer to the prayer of simplicity. A bonus for all is the needed advice given on the problem of lack of concentration in prayer.

Now being read eagerly by lay Christians as well as religious, *Union with the Lord in Prayer* forms the basis for retreats, is used in convents, seminaries, prayer groups and particularly in Sister Formation on three continents. The reasonable paperback format of this indispensable book permits each to have a personal copy. $.75

For both traditional and charismatic lay Christians . . . the mature religious . . . those in Formation . . . seminarians . . . retreatants . . . students.

Some of many comments received:

"*I am especially grateful for Union with the Lord in Prayer. It fills a need for something clear and encouraging on mental prayer which I can use for the novitiate. It is truly the best I have ever come across for the purpose.*"—Sister M. Seraphim, P. C., Sancta Clara Monastery, Canton, Ohio.

"*A magnificent piece of work. It touches on all the essential points of Contemplative Prayer—which is an enormous subject in itself. Yet to bring such a sublime subject down to the level of comprehension of the 'man in the street,' and in such an encouraging way that he or she will not be repelled by the very thought of Contemplative Prayer.*"—Abbott James Fox, O. C. S. O. (former superior of Thomas Merton at the Abbey of Gethsemani).

"*Thank you for making Father Vernard's book available. We think it's beautiful.*"—Rev. Charles Antekier, leader of St. Mary's Prayer Group (Charismatic), Grand Rapids, Mich.

"*Everyone raves over the booklet! I think it is splendid. Makes 'talking with Jesus' so easy.*"—Sister M. Inez, S. B. S., Mission Center, Philadelphia, Pa.

"*We would like to call your attention to an excellent*

little work on prayer, a new book by Father Venard Poslusney, O. Carm. His work is most interesting and readable."—Mary (Aylesford News), Carmelite Third Order publication.

"I find it to be an answer to our present need—for religious, both young and old—for beginners as well as veterans. Congratulations!"—Mother M. Amadeus, Provincial, Felician Sisters, Lodi, N. J.

"The major effort of this little work is to tie in some of the recent charismatic manifestations and experiences found among some Catholics today with the classical experience of prayer described in the doctors of the spiritual live, namely, St. John of the Cross and St. Teresa of Avila."—Cross and Crown Magazine

Attaining Spiritual Maturity for Contemplation 85¢

Union with the Lord in Prayer 75¢

available at your bookstore, or write to

LIVING FLAME PRESS
Box 74
Locust Valley, N. Y. 11560

GATHERED FOR POWER
By Graham Pulkingham
Introduction by Michael Harper

The church that *Guideposts* picked as its church of the year for 1972, and that CBS did a special on, did not start off that way. When Graham Pulkingham inherited the Church of the Redeemer in Houston, it was as dead as it is possible for an Episcopal cathedral to be. Powerless to change it, he sought out David Wilkerson in despair, received the Baptism in the Holy Spirit, and let God use him to build His church His way.

MB-1 SOFTCOVER $2.50

THE HOLY SPIRIT AND YOU
By Dennis and Rita Bennett

As Dennis Bennett emerged as one of the leading teachers and spokesmen of the charismatic renewal, he became increasingly aware of the need for a sound book of teaching on the Baptism in the Holy Spirit — its scriptural basis and historical precedents, what it and the gifts of the Spirit are all about, how one goes about receiving them, and what comes afterwards. So he and his wife Rita set about writing one. The result is a relaxed, clearly written, and comprehensive presentation that has been widely adopted for course use in Christian colleges and may be the best single book on the subject in print.

C-204 HARDCOVER $4.95
L-324 SOFTCOVER $2.50

HOLY SPIRIT AND YOU
TEACHING MANUAL

This is a special supplementary teaching manual, for classroom, group and personal use.

P-031 SOFTCOVER $1.25

LORD OF THE VALLEYS
By Florence Bulle
Introduction by Bob Mumford

What do you do when the hurt is so deep, the pain so excruciating, or the grief so numbing that you cannot pray? What do you do when you begin to wonder where God is; doesn't He know how much you need Him, right now? The agony is real — is His love?

Florence Bulle has had to be hospitalized for a critical lung condition more than forty times, frequently for radical chest surgery. Time after time she has been in blinding pain at the brink of death, only to find her Savior there and have Him take her by the hand and gently lead her back. She has learned how to fellowship with Him, not just on the mountain tops but in the valleys, even in the very pit of despair, and how to lean on Him and climb to victory.

Florence Bulle, a housewife and mother in Houghton, New York, has authored articles in *The American Weekly, Christian Life, The War Cry, Sunday Digest, Power, Fellowship,* and *Home Life.*

L-018 SOFTCOVER $2.50

THEY LEFT THEIR NETS
by W. Graham Pulkingham

Here are the individual stories of many of the lives who make up the community of the Church of the Redeemer in Houston, Texas. This little group who first felt called together in and by the Spirit all give their testimony to the effective and wonderful working of God in their lives when they came into contact with and then became part of this community which transformed a dying, inner-city church into a dynamo of Christian witness and mission.

As author W. Graham Pulkingham says, "It was a community called forth by prophetic visions and established by the authority of our radical commitment to one another in love; we found no need for a covenant agreement or for a charter or for rules. Love was the rule by which we lived."

MB-2 SOFTCOVER $2.50

GOD'S LIVING ROOM
By Herb Walker
with Irene Burk Harrell
Introduction by David Wilkerson

The remarkable story of the Teen Challenge coffee-house ministry to Greenwich Village, directed by Herb and Lucile Walker. Their story has captured the heartache, the danger, the despair — and the victories — of street ministry, and gives powerful evidence of the impossible miracles God will perform when we give Him a chance. A book of excitement and drama, but keynoted by a costly compassion, as the Lord grants them love sufficient to extend His hand to the most hopeless derelict and confused youth to invite them into God's Living Room.

A-123   POCKET PAPER $.95

HEAR MY CONFESSION
By Father Joseph Orsini

What happens when a young Catholic priest with a brilliant mind begins to question the relevance of the Church today, the hypocrisy in himself and his fellow priests, the very divinity of Christ? What happens is usually a downward-spiraling, ever deepening depression that eventually results in either passivity or violent activisim and rebellion. Or quitting the priesthood altogether. On the verge of the latter was where Joe Orsini and the Lord found each other.

Father Orsini is Associate Pastor of the Church of St. Edward in Pine Hill, New Jersey. He is the National Chaplain of Unico National, an Italian-American service organization. He holds a B.A. in Classical languages, and an M.A. in secondary education from Seton Hall and recently received an Ed.D. in Philosophy of Education from Rutgers University.

L-341   POCKET PAPER $1.00
S-407   SPANISH EDITION $ .95
I-413   ITALIAN EDITION $ .95

A NEW WAY OF LIVING
by Michael Harper

This book is about the men and women who make up the fellowship of the Church of the Redeemer, an Episcopal Church in Houston, Texas, who have pioneered a new way of living.

In eight years the church has undergone an astonishing transformation. In 1963 the church had about 900 people on its books, but the majority were inactive, so far as the vital life of the church was concerned. Today average weekly attendance at services is around 2200. How all this came about is quite a story.

But the major contribution that the Church of the Redeemer has made to the Church at large is that it has demonstrated that the practice and experience of community can be easily available to everyone. Community is not easy. But this church has shown that it need no longer only be practiced by a few dreamy-eyed idealists; nor need it be something special and removed from the rest of the Church.

H-070   HARDCOVER $4.95
P-066   SOFTCOVER $2.50